THE
BATTLE
of
THE ALAMO

A HISTORY PERSPECTIVES BOOK

Peggy Caravantes

Published in the United States of America by Cherry Lake Publishing
Ann Arbor, Michigan
www.cherrylakepublishing.com

Consultants: Charles David Grear, PhD, Associate Professor of History,
Prairie View A&M University; Marla Conn, ReadAbility, Inc.
Editorial direction: Red Line Editorial
Book design and illustration: Sleeping Bear Press

Photo Credits: Percy Moran/Library of Congress, cover (left), 1 (left), 4;
Bain News Service/Library of Congress, cover (middle), 1 (middle), 16;
Library of Congress, cover (right), 1 (right), 24; North Wind/North Wind
Picture Archives, 7, 9, 18, 20, 23, 30; C. Stuart/Library of Congress, 13;
Rose West Photo/Shutterstock Images, 26

Library of Congress Cataloging-in-Publication Data

Caravantes, Peggy, 1935-
  The Battle of the Alamo / Peggy Caravantes.
    pages cm. -- (Perspectives library)
  ISBN 978-1-62431-664-7 (hardcover) -- ISBN 978-1-62431-691-3 (pbk.)
-- ISBN 978-1-62431-718-7 (pdf) -- ISBN 978-1-62431-745-3 (hosted
ebook)
  1. Alamo (San Antonio, Tex.)--Siege, 1836--Juvenile literature. I. Title.

  F390.C27 2013
  976.4'03--dc23
                          2013029375

Cherry Lake Publishing would like to acknowledge the work of
The Partnership for 21st Century Skills. Please visit *www.p21.org*
for more information.

Printed in the United States of America
Corporate Graphics Inc.
January 2014

TABLE OF CONTENTS

In this book, you will read about the Battle of the Alamo from three perspectives. Each perspective is based on real things that happened to real people who were involved in or experienced the battle. As you'll see, the same event can look different depending on one's point of view.

1

Peter Evans
Texan Commander

I am a captain in the Texan army and one of the commanders at the Alamo in San Antonio, Texas. The Alamo was originally a **mission** built in the early 1700s. The missionaries there brought Christianity to the Native Americans. Now it serves as a fort for our Texan army in the Texas Revolution. Today is March 6, 1836, and we have been fighting the Mexicans here at the Alamo for 13 days.

The Texas Revolution can trace its roots back to 1824. That year, the territory of Texas became a Mexican state. Most of Texas consisted of American settlers living here on land grants from the Mexican government. We were content to live under Mexico's rules until Antonio López de Santa Anna became Mexico's president in 1833. He ignored his country's **constitution** and made new laws of his own. Mexican states were losing their power, and we were losing our say in the government. This angered us. We were also far away from Mexico City, where the government was located. We decided to **rebel** by trying to break away from Mexico. On October 2, 1835, shots were fired between Mexican soldiers and the people of Gonzales, Texas. This was the start of the Texas Revolution.

SECOND SOURCE

▶ Find a second source that discusses the reasons behind the Texas Revolution. Compare the information in that source to what you read here.

In late 1835, Santa Anna sent General Martín Perfecto de Cós to stop our rebellion. On December 5, Cós's army clashed with a group of 400 Texans here in San Antonio. At that time, the Mexican soldiers had control of the Alamo. Cós turned the Alamo into a fort by placing 21 cannons at the site. The Mexican soldiers fought our army from behind its walls. But we won. Then we moved into the Alamo. We were hoping we could protect San Antonio from within its walls. We needed to make sure the Mexicans did not take control of the city. It is an important stop on the road that connects eastern and southern Texas.

After we defeated General Cós, we tried to create a stronger defense at the mission. Colonel James C. Neill was put in charge of the Alamo's defense. We took stock of the area. The Alamo was a three-acre complex with a large open square in its center. Limestone walls about eight feet tall and four feet thick surrounded the complex. On the north and west sides, small buildings on the inside braced the outer walls. A low **barracks** supported the southern wall. On the east side was a two-story structure called the Long Barrack. About 50 yards from that building was the chapel, and at the back was the horse corral.

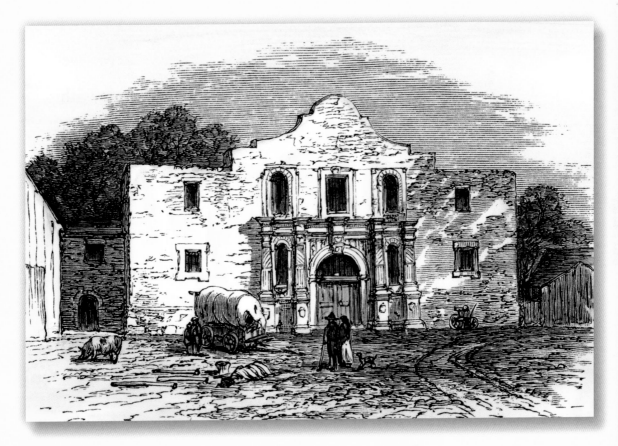

▲ *The Alamo served as a mission before it became a Texan army fort.*

Our first task was to brace the walls damaged in our battle with General Cós. We were piling hills of dirt to mount our cannons on when Colonel James Bowie arrived on January 19, 1836. He carried orders from Major General Sam Houston of the Texan army to destroy the Alamo. After all our hard work, the news shocked us. General Houston knew the Alamo was a weak defense. He thought we should retreat to Gonzales, which was roughly 70 miles east. It was easier to protect than the Alamo and San Antonio. Plus, it could serve as an alternate trade route. If we left, we would have to abandon our heavy weapons. Houston did not want us to leave arms for the enemy. His solution was to blow up the whole mission.

Colonel Neill wanted to stay at the Alamo. He convinced Colonel Bowie that protecting San Antonio was critical. We could stop Santa Anna at San Antonio if he decided to march toward Texas's

▲ *General Houston was a leader in the Texan army during the Texas Revolution.*

northern borders. Colonel Bowie agreed. They ignored Houston's order. We would defend the Alamo.

Colonel Bowie became one of our commanders. Colonel Neill had to leave on February 11 because of a family illness. Colonel Neill chose Lieutenant Colonel William Barret Travis to take his commanding position. Colonel Bowie and Colonel Travis clashed over leadership

DAVY CROCKETT

Davy Crockett was born in 1786. He was a frontiersman and a successful politician. He served in the U.S. Congress in the 1820s and the 1830s. Books written about him told of a larger-than-life hero of the West. He remains a popular character in American folklore.

but finally agreed to share the command. About that same time, Davy Crockett arrived from Tennessee with 12 more men. He encouraged the commanders to assign tasks to make our defense stronger.

In early February, scouts brought news that Santa Anna was headed toward San Antonio with an army of 3,000 to 4,000 soldiers. Colonel Travis told us to prepare for an assault. I ordered my men to be sure their rifles, shotguns, pistols, and knives were ready. Then I sent them to work on the tasks the colonels had assigned. Some repaired the damaged north wall. Others dug defensive ditches around the outer southern walls. We hoped this would prevent enemy soldiers from getting over our walls. Those who dug the ditches used the dug-up earth to build raised areas to mount the cannons and to brace other walls. Another group chopped up iron horseshoes to use in the cannons.

Santa Anna and his army arrived in San Antonio on February 23. Thousands of Mexican soldiers swarmed into the city. In the distance, we could see the soldiers had hung a red flag on the San Fernando Cathedral. We knew this meant the Mexican army would show no mercy. They would not allow us to **surrender** and keep our lives. They would take no prisoners. Colonel Travis answered with a cannon blast. The battle had begun.

For the first four days, the attacks were constant. Although we were greatly outnumbered, our band of nearly 200 men within the Alamo held steady. With well-placed shots, we stopped the enemy soldiers from moving their cannons closer to the outer walls. At night, they kept us awake with cannon blasts and bugle calls. During this time, Colonel Bowie became terribly ill. On February 24, he turned over his command to Colonel Travis.

Two days later, we stopped returning fire. We needed to preserve the small supply of ammunition we had left. Colonel Travis sent out pleas for help to the people of Gonzales. The Mexican army let the **couriers** through for several days. On March 1, 32 men arrived from Gonzales and at 3:00 a.m. slipped into the Alamo under cover of darkness. Despite our hope for larger numbers, no more came.

I tried to keep my men's spirits up. They realized our situation was **bleak**. The enemy attacks

▲ *Crockett left his home in Tennessee to join the fight against Mexico in the Texas Revolution.*

continued until March 5, when no more shots were fired. There was dead silence. Colonel Travis called us together. He knew Santa Anna was getting ready for a major assault. He explained we could surrender and later be killed or we could fight to the death. Using his sword, he drew a line in the courtyard dirt. He stepped across it. Then he invited all who planned to stay and fight to step over the line. One by one the men joined him. Colonel Bowie asked some men to carry his stretcher across the line. We vowed to make the Mexicans remember the Alamo.

Then the Mexican bugles sounded *el degüello*, the cry for murder. I ordered my men to their posts. The riflemen lay on top of the walls, making them easy targets. Colonel Travis joined them and fired his rifle. He was hit in the forehead by a single lead ball and died instantly. I raced to take his place, but suddenly hundreds of Mexican soldiers were climbing over the north wall. I ran toward the Long

Barrack at the east wall. My comrades and I fought with knives and guns as we fled.

We had prepared the Long Barrack by digging ditches in the dirt floor. As we got to the barracks, we fired through holes in the wall and from behind barriers made from cowhide to provide some protection. We forgot that the deserted cannons could be used against us. As the barracks doors closed behind me, I looked back. Some Mexican soldiers were already swinging our north wall cannon around. They aimed it right at us.

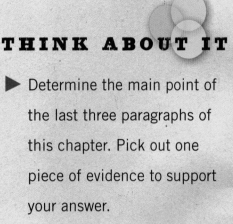

THINK ABOUT IT

▶ Determine the main point of the last three paragraphs of this chapter. Pick out one piece of evidence to support your answer.

Manuel Vela

Mexican Soldier

My name is Manuel Vela. I joined General Santa Anna's army when it passed through my village in Mexico. He was going to stop the Texan rebels, who were trying to break away from Mexico. He said if we loved Mexico, we must protect it. We must also punish the Texans for killing our comrades during General Cós's defeat in San Antonio. I marched for two months to reach San Antonio.

As we neared the Alamo, we remembered our comrades' blood that was spilled there only a few months ago. Despite being tired, hungry, and cold, and having blisters on our feet, we were ready to fight. The rebels must have spotted us, because we heard the bells of the Alamo church ringing a warning. Santa Anna sent a few men ahead to raise our red flag. That told the Texans there would be no mercy. They answered with a cannon shot. The battle had started.

THINK ABOUT IT

▶ Determine the main point of this paragraph. Select one piece of evidence that supports your answer.

We shot at the Alamo walls while our army bands played loud military music to encourage us. The Texans didn't want us to move closer. They peppered us with rifle fire and more cannon blasts. We moved back for a while.

On the second night of fighting, a few of our **cavalry** attacked the rear of the fort near the horse

▲ *The Mexican army traveled many miles to reach San Antonio and the Alamo.*

corrals. The Texans saw us, and we had to retreat. The exchange of gunfire and cannon shots lasted for several days. Then on February 26, the enemy stopped firing. My fellow soldiers and I just wanted to wait them out. We knew they must not have much firepower left. They would give up soon.

On March 5, General Santa Anna decided he didn't want to wait anymore. He told the other generals to prepare for an early morning attack the next day. To get ready, we assembled ladders for climbing over the walls. We gathered crowbars and axes for breaking through any locked doors.

Our commanders made us go to bed at dusk. At midnight, they woke us up to prepare for the attack.

ANTONIO LÓPEZ DE SANTA ANNA

Born in 1794, Santa Anna began his military career at age 16. He became a national hero during Mexico's fight for freedom from Spain, which lasted from 1810 to 1821. Mexicans elected him president in 1833. After his victory at the Alamo, General Houston's army defeated him at San Jacinto in the territory of Texas. His loss led to Texas becoming an independent republic.

◀ *Santa Anna was the Mexican president and a military leader.*

We were divided into four columns. Each column, headed by a general, would attack one side of the Alamo. By 3:00 a.m., we were gathered 300 feet from the fort, waiting for the signal. We had stopped firing on the Texans several hours before. Now there was nothing but silence. At 5:30 a.m., we received the command to attack. The Texans were ready for us and fired back. They pushed us back time and time again. More than 40 of my comrades died around me.

I was located on the north side of the Alamo. I helped place a ladder, but it was not tall enough. We climbed the rest of the way inside the mission on one another's backs. As we tumbled over the walls, we shouted, "Long live the Mexican Republic!" We fought hand to hand with the Texan soldiers we met inside. They used knives, and their guns served as clubs.

Many of the defenders rushed toward a long building on the east side and bolted the doors behind them. My comrades and I swung the north wall cannon around and fired it at them. From their hiding places, some of the Texans extended white surrender cloths. They indicated they wanted to give up. We tried to accept the offers, only to be shot at by other Texans who did not plan to surrender. This increased our fury, and new fights broke out. After a little more than an hour, the battle inside the Alamo was over. The Texan soldiers were all dead. The 13-day battle was over. We walked around the Alamo's grounds to make sure no soldiers were hiding. In the chapel, we found a few

ANALYZE THIS

▶ Compare the perspectives of the Texan commander and the Mexican soldier. Are they alike in any ways? How so? How are they different?

Tejanas, several of their children, and a white woman and her baby girl.

Santa Anna told a soldier who spoke a little English to call for any African-American slaves to show themselves. A few men came out of hiding. One soldier poked one with his **bayonet**, while another soldier shot another slave with his gun. But a captain stopped them from further hurting the slaves. He made the slaves show him the bodies of the Texan leaders. After that, he sent the white woman and her baby with one of the African-American men to tell General Houston what to expect from the Mexican army. He ordered the other African Americans be kept as prisoners. After questioning the Tejanas, he released them.

Then we piled nearly 200 dead rebel bodies on two funeral **pyres** and set fire to them. By early evening of March 6, 1836, black smoke hid the sky over San Antonio. It had been a horrible **massacre**. We lost about 600 men and took the time to bury them.

If the Texans had obeyed our laws, everybody would have been better off.

▲ *The Mexican army outnumbered the Texan army soldiers and was able to take control of the Alamo.*

3

Ned

Surviving Slave

My name is Ned, and I have been a slave all my life. This morning, I walked through a wet field around the horse corral when I fed the animals. I was cleaning mud off my shoes when I heard loud shouts outside the Alamo walls. "Viva Santa Anna! Viva la República!" I knew the enemy was here. I shook my master, one of the soldiers here. He woke up and grabbed his sword and double-barreled shotgun. He yelled for me to bring the other guns and follow him.

We reached one of the outer walls of the complex. My master climbed on top of the wall and started shooting at the enemy. Others got ready to fire the cannons. Women and children hid in the church. The Mexicans played loud bugles outside the walls.

There was nothing to hide the men on top of the wall. My master lay down on his stomach and fired his rifle. My job was to reload the guns he used. Outside the walls, Mexican soldiers crowded together. In the distance, I saw their red flag on the tower of the San Fernando Cathedral.

Wounded and dying men from both sides yelled in pain. Colonel Travis was on the wall next to my master. A lead ball hit

SECOND SOURCE

▶ Find another source about a slave who survived at the Alamo. Compare the information in that source to the information in this chapter.

▲ *The Mexican army hung their red flag on the San Fernando Cathedral.*

Colonel Travis in the head. Shortly after that, my master was killed. I grabbed a shotgun and ran. I hid in one of the mission's small buildings. Its walls had little holes that I could look through. When I stopped shaking, I fired my gun. Then I quit. The soldiers inside the mission used hand-to-hand fighting with pistols, knives, and swords. It was so crowded that shots often went wild, killing fellow soldiers instead of enemies.

The Mexican soldiers just kept coming. They climbed over all the walls to get inside the mission. I quit watching and hid behind some bushels of corn in the corner. I hated the terrible screams of pain. Sounds of the enemy soldiers were everywhere. I heard them chopping at walls and doors with their axes. There was a blast to the building next door. They were shooting the Texan army's cannons at us. When the gunfire stopped, I looked out one more time. Bodies covered the ground. I expected to be killed any minute.

A man entered through the big gate. He wore a fancy black- and-red uniform with gold

ANALYZE THIS

▶ Analyze the accounts of the Mexican assault on the Alamo as seen from the viewpoints of the Texan commander and the surviving slave. How are they different? How are they the same?

braids. He carried a shining sword. The Mexican soldiers saluted him. He must have been their leader. He said something to one of his soldiers. That man shouted for any slaves in hiding to come out. I was scared, but I obeyed the order. I screamed when one Mexican soldier poked my side with a knife. Another man in a fancier uniform made him stop. A few other slaves came out from different buildings. I couldn't believe I was still alive—at least for now.

I heard the Mexicans call the man in the bright uniform Santa Anna. He made us show him the bodies of Travis, Bowie, and Crockett. He talked to some women who had been hiding in the chapel. I knew one of the ladies. I helped her move her things into the church. She was Susanna Dickinson. She was holding her baby close to her chest.

Now Santa Anna has ordered Mrs. Dickinson and me to go to Gonzales, where General Houston is. He said we are to tell Houston he should expect this kind of defeat from the Mexican army. I hope

Houston and his army act accordingly. I don't think

I can take seeing another massacre like this one.

SUSANNA DICKINSON

At age 15, Susanna Wilkerson of Tennessee married Almeron Dickinson. Soon after, they moved to Texas. Her husband, one of the Alamo defenders, died in the battle. Susanna and her baby, Angelina, were among the few survivors. Susanna was the only white settler to be an eyewitness to the last moments of the battle.

LOOK, LOOK AGAIN

Look closely at this picture of the Battle of the Alamo and answer the following questions:

1. What would a Texan Alamo defender notice most in this picture? Would he be encouraged or discouraged? Why?

2. How would a Mexican soldier describe this picture to his friends when he returned to Mexico?

3. What would a slave within the Alamo think about when he saw this picture?

GLOSSARY

barracks (BAR-uhks) a building or a group of buildings that soldiers live in

bayonet (BAY-uh-net) a long blade that can fit over the end of a rifle and serve as a weapon

bleak (BLEEK) unlikely to have a positive outcome

cavalry (KAV-uhl-ree) the part of an army that fought while on horses

couriers (KUR-ee-urs) messengers

massacre (MAS-uh-kur) the violent killing of a number of people at the same time, often in battle

mission (MISH-uhn) a church or other place where missionaries work

pyres (PYRS) heaps of wood for burning a dead body

rebel (ri-BEL) to fight against authority, especially the authority of one's government

surrender (suh-REN-duhr) to give up or to stop resisting someone or something

Tejanas (tay-HAH-nuhs) women having Texan and Mexican ancestry

LEARN MORE

Further Reading

Murphy, Jim. *Inside the Alamo.* New York: Delacorte Press, 2003.
Tanaka, Shelley. *The Alamo: Surrounded and Outnumbered, They Chose to Make a Defiant Last Stand.* New York: Hyperion Books for Children, 2003.
Walker, Paul Robert. *Remember the Alamo: Texians, Tejanos, and Mexicans Tell Their Stories.* Washington, DC: National Geographic, 2007.

Web Sites

The Alamo
http://www.history.com/topics/alamo
This Web site has more history of the Alamo, including several videos.

Battle of the Alamo
http://www.thealamo.org/
This Web site has more background information on the Battle of the Alamo as well as several activities for kids.

INDEX

ABOUT THE AUTHOR

Peggy Caravantes, a retired educator, is the author of several nonfiction books for students of all ages. She lives in San Antonio, Texas, the home of the Alamo. She also wrote *The Orphan Trains*, another title in the History Perspectives series.